She
and the
World Laughs
with Her

By
Dr. Ann E. Weeks

Design & illustrations by
Moonlight Graphic Works / Stephen Sebree

PASSAGES PUBLISHING, INC.
Louisville, Kentucky

She Laughs and the World Laughs with Her

Passages Publishing, Inc.
P.O. Box 5093
Louisville, KY 40205

Library of Congress Catalog Number
95-70771

ISBN 1-886036-07-1
Printed in the United States

Acknowledgment

Thanks goes to. . .
My editor, Bob Roddy,
who generously shares his talent and time.
Eileen Foot, my daughter, and Jean, my daughter-in-law, for
their proof-reading skills.
Jenny and Patty for all the hours and patience.
Clark for his appreciation and encouragement of the laughter.
The women who generously contributed their stories –
thanks for showing us the way.

Dedication

To the special women in my life with whom I laugh –
Eileen, Theresa, Jean, Beth and Susan.

Life does not cease to be funny
when someone dies, anymore than it ceases
to be serious when someone laughs

George Bernard Shaw

Contents

Wake Up Calls and More...

I am a nurse and have loved nursing since I was ten. I was the classic case of the idealistic gal who had read all of the *Cherry Ames: Nurse* books and dreamed of being the heroine.

I have followed that early dream and then some. I was the first Dean of the School of Nursing, Education and Health Sciences at Bellarmine College in Louisville, Kentucky. Today, I am a nurse family therapist in private practice, an author, and a national speaker.

To most people it would seem that I had realized my dreams and should be well satisfied to spend my middle-age years enjoying the fulfillment of all that I had hoped for. But that has proved not to be the case. Chasing dreams and listening to that inner voice has not yet finished. In fact, that inner voice continues to be the hallmark of my life. Following my dreams and listening to my intuitions have led me into wonderful opportunities - and sometimes a bit of hot water.

In 1982, I experienced the first feelings of career burnout. While I still enjoyed being a nurse therapist and teaching students, I found myself less and less tolerant of all the tin gods. I've never been very much of a rule follower and most enjoyed the creative, innovative part of any job. Routine, regulations, rules and rigidity were beginning to stifle me.

Then my life took several dramatic turns that caused me to evaluate who I was and how I wanted to spend the rest of my working days. This life review was made more immediate by four wake-up calls.

The media frequently features stories about individuals being given a sign, a "wake-up call," to go in another direction. Sometimes the wake-up call comes in the form of a personal setback or a near death experience. I didn't receive just one call but a whole series over a six year period of time. I was so caught up in my life that I minimized the first two of the four wake-up calls. Wake-up calls three and four finally got my attention.

1983 found me happily married with three children. I was a full-time member of the nursing faculty at Bellarmine College. I also had a therapy practice part-time. If that wasn't enough, I was doing doctoral work at Indiana University School of Nursing in Indianapolis. A workaholic's fantasy!

That year my father had extensive surgery for cancer. I took a semester off from doctoral studies to help my mother care for him. Fourteen months later he died - wake-up call number one.

Ten weeks after Dad died, my mother had a massive stroke that left her wheelchair bound. My brothers and sisters and I took turns taking care of her...wake-up call number two.

Wake-up call number three came five years later in 1989. My beloved first husband, Paul Kleine-Kracht, had a stroke at age 51. I finally began to reorder the priorities in my life. I resigned my position as Dean to spend more time with him. In September, 1990 Paul suffered a second stroke and died. WAKE-UP CALL NUMBER FOUR.

I was 50 years old and all of a sudden nothing seemed as important as it had. The grief, mingled with the ever growing burnout, made me realize that I had to do something different. But there was the reality of "How would I support myself and my two children who remained at home?" My frustration and impatience grew. I found myself trapped; focusing only on the closed doors. Then one day I reminded myself to look for the open window that is always there when one door closes.

Two years after Paul's death I met a wonderful man and widower, Clark Weeks. He helped me in my search for the open window. He suggested that I slow down and enjoy life. He listened and encouraged me to get serious about being who I wanted to be. I came to realize that I had to take some risks to achieve my dream because there are no guarantees about tomorrows.

I married Clark in September, 1993. I am still very busy but am now doing what I enjoy the most: speaking, writing and counseling. Clark and I travel frequently to places where I tell stories, make people laugh and refocus their lives.

I know that most of us don't relish wake-up calls; they jar us from the comfort of our daily existence and force us to face something new and uncertain. But the wake-up call holds the promise of something new; perhaps more suited to the current leanings of our heart and spirit. And, through it all I realized the importance of humor in coping.

This book is the result of an invitation I made to women to share their stories of coping with life's events with humor. I wanted these women to tell others how they were better able to deal with a wake-up call because of a funny remark, someone's humorous actions or just a silly thought.

After all, humor is a integral part of an individual's sense of well being. Research has found that playfulness, spontaneity and humor encourage high levels of creativity, achievement and physical and mental health. Humor is such a positive dimension in our lives because it exists for the pleasure it gives a person without a price tag. It has been said that a person without a sense of humor is like a wagon without springs - jolted by every pebble on life's road. I hope that these stories provide some "springs" for the rocky moments in your life as well.

The Appliance Man Ringeth

One of the many challenges that I was confronted with after my first husband's death was people calling and asking to speak to him. Paul was an attorney and calls from clients and others unaware of his death continued for months.

One evening a couple of months after Paul's death the phone rang."Hello, Kleine-Kracht's residence," I stated.

"May I speak to Paul Kleine-Kracht?" he said. I caught my breath and said, "I'm sorry Paul is deceased. I'm his wife, may I help you?"

Without any comment about what I'd just said, the caller jumped right in with, "I'm John Jones with the Appliance Warranty Center. I'm calling to remind you that your warranty on your appliance is about to expire and you need to renew it."

"Thank you for calling, but that appliance is several years old and I've decided not to renew the warranty."

With a tone of impatience, he responded, "Well, I'm

4

sure your dead husband would want you to renew."

My humor and coping clicked in as I replied, "Funny you should mention it, but just hours before Paul died he said, Honey, whatever you do, don't renew the appliance warranty!"

There was silence and then Mr. Jones said, "Oh, oh okay, and hung up.

A. W.

An Irish Lass

I'd like to share one woman's story and her use of humor to cope with life. She was the second of five children in a Irish-German family. She claimed only the Irish heritage because she maintained they were the fun loving side of her family.

This woman was a teenager during the Great Depression. She wasn't able to finish school because there were more pressing needs in the family. As a young woman, she experienced the great midwestern flood of 1937 and married that same year. Her husband should have lived a hundred years earlier because he saw himself as a pioneer and thus did everything the hard way because he enjoyed the challenge.

After forty-seven years of marriage, five children, the death of both parents and the death of her husband, this women suffered a life-changing stroke. She was unable to walk independently, drive a car, or live by herself. She hated all the adjustment this meant and most of all her lack of freedom. She was above all things a survivor, sometimes a reluctant one, but a survivor none the less.

Her use of humor was always there, however. During her all-too-frequent trips to the hospital, she would always use one of the following comments with the hospital personnel:

"Don't you think it's terrible that a woman of my age is pregnant and needs to be in the hospital?"

"I got hurt snow skiing. That's why I'm in this wheelchair!"

"I'm going dancing later. Don't wait up."

"I've got a date with some motorcyclists to go for a ride."

Because she was elderly, had gray hair and was in a wheelchair, the person would look at her like she was disoriented and confused. She'd wait for this reaction and then give a laugh and say, "I'm just teasing." She loved to catch people with her outrageous comments.

This woman was my mother and she died June 30, 1994 at the age of 77. Rest in the peace of Christ, Mother. You can wear your high heels now!

A. W.

Please Pass the Salad Dressing

Raising seven children can be pretty hectic to say the least and sometimes quite complicated. At one time my husband and I had seven children in five schools on three shifts and my husband was working the swing shift. There were many times when a sense of humor helped us over some of the rough spots.

One evening, my husband was working the afternoon and evening shift. The kids and I were eating our evening meal which was pretty noisy as usual. This was the time when they all wanted to talk about their day, tell jokes, tease one another. Just your normal, suppertime chaos.

It had been one of those days. I was really tired and the children could sense the tension. I just wanted to get the meal over with.

I was sitting at the head of the table and my daughter, Mary, was sitting on my right. Before she put salad dressing on her salad, she picked up the bottle and gave it a good hard shake. The cap flew off the bottle and the French dressing hit me "splat" in the face! The orange, oily "goop" slid down my nose, covered my glasses and dripped off my chin. As I looked out through the orange haze there was dead silence.

My oldest daughter, Amanda, began to shake a little. I warned her, "Don't you laugh!"

For a second she didn't, then she couldn't hold it any longer; she got up from the table and went into the living room where she lay down on the living room floor. The

rest of the kids drifted away from the tables to their various chores; dishes, garbage, homework, baths, etc. Throughout the evening I could hear snickers and giggles and by bed time all was calm.

When Jim came home I told him the story and we both laughed about it. Since then, as the years have passed, I realize more and more that the humor in this story helped me get past the daily grind.

It's a story that can be told when we are all together, and still gets a big laugh and gives me a warm feeling especially on a day when I'm missing the kids.

They're all grown now, and needing a little cheer...

There are a lot of funny stories about each of the kids, but for some reason this one seems to come to mind real often as though there is a message there. If there is, I hope I have learned it because our home has been filled with much love and laughter.

A.B.

Frightening Relief

At home on the farm when I was a child, we did not have an indoor bathroom but a full fledged, outdoor, "double-seater." It was a nice little outhouse, painted white with a real working knob that operated from both sides. It sat on a hill behind the meat house with flowers, bushes, pear and cherry trees all around. In the summertime there were also lots of tall weeds. It had good ventilation because it didn't smell as bad as the ones at some of my friends' and relatives' homes.

Each night, after the dishes were done and my homework was completed, I vividly remember my visit before bed. It was usually getting dark at the time of my last trip out. Bravely, I would walk out the back door, down the steps to the path by the meat house where the hams and bacon hung to smoke and cure. Sausage and other pig parts were also stored there right after hog killing.

I did not like to think of those unsavory morsels, like pigs' feet, heads and tails. They were not gourmet delights that I could be challenged to partake of! I remember once when my uncle, who lived with us, put a long, greasy, hairy pig tail on my plate and told me to eat it!! He smiled with delight as I cried and squirmed in horror.

I would pass the brown clapped board building and was delighted to find no one standing behind it. I always looked!

I remember how the wind whistled around the little building, and farm sounds could be heard in the piercing darkness. The cows would intermittently moan, while the pigs snorted and the crickets chirped. Always I approached this little establishment with honest bravery and entered with no fear.

10

After completing the task at hand, I would leave
immediately, never lingering to try to identify all the
sounds that surrounded me. I would walk out slowly, turn
the knob to secure the door and start my long journey back
to the house. Why was the path so much longer going
back than it was coming? How could it get so dark in just
the few minutes that it took me to complete this necessary
task? As I marched forward, it was then that the
unexpected, overwhelming fear would start!!

"I must get in the house. I can't stay out here all night,
heaven forbid! I have to walk by myself - no one is going
to come out to hold my hand. Why do the lights in the
house seem so far away? Maybe if my bladder was bigger

11

I could have waited until morning. That's history now, so come on feet just walk!"

And they would, that is until they turned the corner around that smoky old meat house. Then I would start to run and run like no other time in my life. It was like all the world was behind me, ready to grab me and take me into the darkness!

"Who will it be? Where will they take me? Will I ever see my family again? Where are the steps? Will I ever feel their elevation again in my life time?"

What a relief when your little feet jump two steps at a time and what a sense of accomplishment when you know you did it once more! Back in the house safely, I would always turn and look proudly and bravely into the darkness and know that once more I had conquered one of the terrors of the night!

That is until tomorrow!!

T.W.

Typo-Laughical Errors

Singing for me has been a great joy. I grew up doing it, and it's in the jeans of my family.

Sex is not something that should be stressed, but it should not be avoided like the plaque.

The soldiers wore "camelflodge" gear.

From papers presented to tutors in the CAI Lab

Mom Needs a Ride

My Mom had been in intensive care for six weeks prior to her death. Needless to say there was not much joy in our lives during the long hospitalization and after her death.

When we received our last call from the hospital, they showed us to a small room to wait for the doctor and to cry, scream, whatever.

Personally, I had never before had to deal with death and this was my Mother!

I sat there thinking, 'Mom is here in the hospital, but now she needs to be at the funeral home.'

I turned to my husband and asked, "How is Mom going to get to the funeral home?"

His startled reply was, "I don't know but she's not riding in our car!"

That one little statement eased the emotions and tension wonderfully and I'll never forget it.

P.S.

13

God's Clock Runs Slow

Your family is scheduled to leave on a 7PM flight to Florida, but the plane is delayed, so you have to change plans and leave a whole day later. It seems to be yet another clog in your hopes that things will go the way you plan. However, your young daughter has time to recover from a pesky stomach virus, and you have the opportunity to spend some unexpected, peaceful hours with your parents. God's clock runs slow.

You lock your keys in the car accidentally as you pack for a 15 hour road trip. You know you have to be on the road by 5AM to keep your schedule for safety which will allow you to arrive at your destination before dark. The next day you read about an accident in which a sixteen-wheeler careened across the median on I-95 at 5:10AM — the exact time you would have been there if you hadn't had to wait for the locksmith to open your car door. God's clock runs slow.

You are moving from out of state — your first move in 28 years of marriage. That amount of time, coupled with the collections of "stuff" by seven children make a major difference in the amount of time and effort required to pack up and move. Add your inexperience with moving in general; your spouse's work schedule which demands that he be gone until three days before the actual move; your son's wedding (IN THE OLD HOMETOWN) just three weeks after the move, and finally the fact that the new house is going to be 1,000 square feet smaller; you have a fairly good recipe for stress!

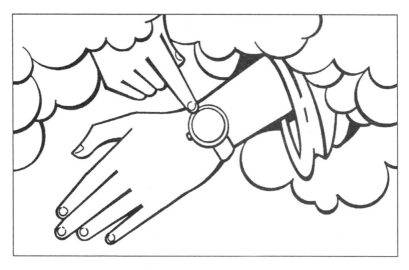

Just when all the logistics seem to be in place, you decide to order some new stationery with the new address imprinted to save time with change-of-address letters. Thirty-two hours after you mail the order, your husband calls to inform you that a roomier house with a garage — located 145 miles north of your "other" new house — has become available, and he is in the process of signing the lease. At that moment, all you can think of is the 500 pieces of printed stationery headed for the wrong place.

The last-minute change in plans saves the family $400 in moving expenses. Your high-strung pet schnauzer only requires two "doggie downers" for the trip. Your husband scouts the "new, new" neighborhood and finds two houses with pink bicycles in the driveways — a healthy sign that your seven and eight-year old daughters will have playmates. And, best of all, you now have room for the antique, round oak table which has been the site of all the family's major crises and triumphs. God's clock runs slow.

S.D.

I Never Noticed You Were Bald!

My husband is bald and has been since his early 20's.

I was diagnosed with breast cancer and was told I would lose my hair within 2 weeks of my first chemotherapy treatment.

On the 12th day, I washed my hair and it started coming out by the handfuls. I became hysterical!!!

My husband tried to console me and I yelled, "But you don't know what it's like losing your hair and being bald!"

He gently answered, "Look at me. I've been this way for 50 years!"

With that, we laughed, cried and I pulled myself together.

J.A.S.

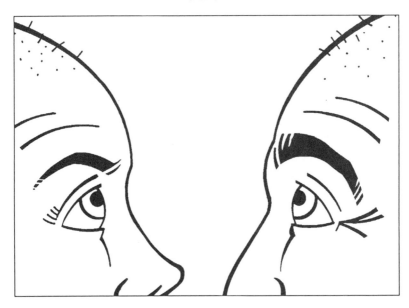

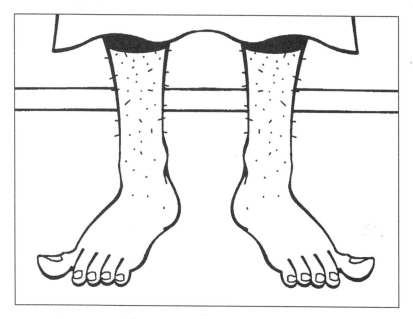

Ready, Set, Oops!

I was told this story by the Occupational Therapist on the scene.

The setting - the cubicle of an ICU patient. Monitors, pumps, lines, drips, binging, beeps, whooshing sounds, ventilator rhythmically breathing, kind of a gentle chaotic atmosphere.

The time had arrived for the patient to GET OUT OF BED for the first time. What a production... the physical therapist is there, the occupational therapist is there, the nurse and two hefty guys from transportation are there. The cast of characters are present and the star of our show is Mr. P.

He wrote on his notepad that he is very nervous about all this. We reassured him everything would be fine. We were there to help him.

I had just finished getting his socks and shoes on. We were ready. Suddenly I blurted out, "WAIT"!!! OH MY GOSH, HIS FEET ARE ON BACKWARDS!"

We all looked down and it was the silliest thing. His feet – actually his shoes – were headed in opposite directions. We cracked up, including the patient who wrote, "Do you do this kind of thing (job) often?"

It really broke the ice, relaxed us all, engaged the patient and brought everything into perspective...just getting out of bed, not diminishing the fact that it was a complex activity.'

The occupational therapist reports, "I'm thinking about making this mistake again"!! Another person sold on the simple yet exquisite rewards of humor!

C. J.

Typo-Laughical Errors

He kept everything in his mental wearhouse.

The Spanish were defeated because of strong navel power.

*One Grecian lady fell in a drunken stupor
after too much parting.*

*Did you know a man falls in love within the first sex
minutes of a first date?*

From papers presented to tutors in the CAI Lab

18

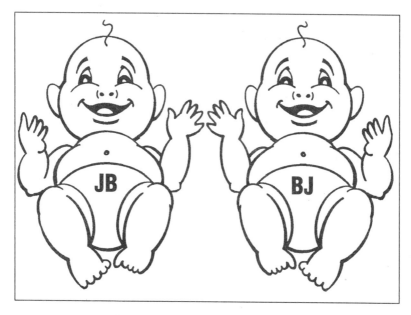

God's Sense of Humor

Having tried unsuccessfully for over eight years, my husband and I were delighted to discover we were expectant parents for a fourth time.

I began to worry, however, when my local doctor suggested that I see a specialist in Louisville, KY so they could better monitor my pregnancy because of my age (43)! Neither my husband, nor myself considered age a problem; after all we still felt young, even though our 17 year old daughter considered us relics.

We had dropped our maternity rider a few years back when we switched insurance companies; we figured that we wouldn't have any more children. We would have to foot all the bills. Thus we decided to forego ultrasound to save money.

Naming the anticipated baby was a big decision. We had a son who was named after his dad and two daughters. We picked out some girls' names pretty easy. But a boy's name was more of a challenge.

You see, ever since I was old enough to plan a family I had wanted a boy named Brian. Finally, this was going to be my chance to have a boy named Brian. But there was a problem. I had a brother named Joseph, who died shortly after birth; my husband and his father also had brothers named Joseph. It was equally important to have a little Joseph in the family.

All through the nine months I tossed and turned, fretted and worried Joseph Brian or Brian Joseph? At nights I would run these names through my head, causing lots of lost sleep.

Finally, my labor began. Surrounded by my husband, 12 year old son and 17 year old daughter, we trooped to the hospital. The doctor decided to do an ultrasound. SURPRISE - TWIN BOYS! 43 years old, no insurance, TWINS!

The first picture of Jesus I saw after bringing Joseph Brian and Brian Joseph home was that of the "Laughing Jesus." His head thrown back in the happiest looking laugh I have ever seen.

My husband and I took one look and roared with laughter too. Who could say God doesn't have a sense of humor?

C.B.

Send in the Clowns

I work in the burn center of a pediatric hospital which includes adult patients in the burn unit. I am 50 years old and have been working with burn patients for 11 years. Due to this type of injury, we use humor frequently to help the patients and to maintain our own morale.

I have chosen to cope by becoming a clown. Our clown group consists of volunteers from various departments in the hospital. We volunteer one evening a month and visit patients and their families.

Our costumes vary. I dress in an exaggerated nurse uniform with red shiny hair, clown make-up, and sequin shoes. I carry a large plastic syringe, thermometer, and like items. We tell jokes, do magic tricks, and whatever is needed to get a smile.

It is amazing the satisfaction I get from seeing a child smile or parents feeling comfortable to talk with a non-threatening clown.

R. T.

I Didn't Know Whether to Laugh or Cry

I was involved in a serious car wreck in February, 1994. I used humor to deal with the pain and frustrations that I encountered in the long months of recovery.

It started immediately when the EMS technician put a board under me and put a cervical collar around my neck to prevent further injury. I joked about getting "a nose job" since my nose was probably broken. I assured him that I was wearing clean underwear. When he asked my age I said, "Guess?". When he guessed at least 10 years my junior, I told him "Thanks for the compliment."

I even joked with my boss, my principal, when I called to inform him of my mishap and explained that I looked like I was wearing a Halloween monster mask. (The airbag had mashed my face and jaw).

Even my doctors and physical therapist couldn't understand how I could act so "up" when I was always in pain. I never wanted anyone to take pity on me. So I laughed to put them at ease.

I often tell my story over and over again, and laugh and crack jokes explaining all I'd been through. I think without the jokes, and making fun of a stressful situation I would probably have cried 24 hours a day for the past 18 months (instead I only cried when I couldn't take any more in my moments of desperation).

I still joke a lot when I recount the events of my past

struggles. Going back to work, seeing friends,
volunteering at a local hospital, and trying to get back to
my fitness routine were all slow in coming, but I am sure
that without my sense of humor I wouldn't have made it
this far.

K.E.D.

What an Entrance!

My dear husband died suddenly and unexpectedly a few days before Christmas. It was a traumatic time for all of us and the evening after we returned from the wake, we were still rather shell-shocked at what had happened.

I was sitting on the couch, with my children on either side of me; we had begun to share family stories to help ease the pain. I looked at my youngest son who was about 15 years old and who had the reputation for being the class clown.

I said, "Jim, did you know that you were born in the elevator of St. Mary's Hospital?"

"WHAAAT!" he exclaimed, "Is that why I'm so colorful?"

"I don't know about that, but I had some problems when I was pregnant with you. When I went into labor I knew that you were coming quickly so I told your dad to just drive and not pay any attention to me, no matter what I said or did. [We lived on a farm about seven miles from town.]"

"I don't know how your dad got us there so quickly. We both just got on the elevator and pushed the button for the maternity floor. When we arrived at the maternity floor of the hospital, your dad pushed the STOP button on the elevator and ran to get some help."

"By the time the Sister and the Nurse arrived, it was too late! You were making your grand entrance on the elevator. You also have to know that I was fully clothed and even had a hat on!"

"The nun was furious. Of course I was so embarrassed at the whole thing.

"Don't you ever come back to this hospital to have a baby unless you're wearing your nightgown!" she admonished. [When I came back three years later to have your sister, I wore my nightgown.]

"Do you want to put her on the OB table, Sister?" the nurse asked.

"NO! No sense getting it dirty with this mess!" Sister replied.

"I was mortified and I could tell that the young nurse felt sorry for me."

"But that's not the half of it. The entire time that I was in the hospital, people kept peering in my room. I later found out that there was a lady who was often in the hospital with heart trouble, and that they usually put her on the maternity floor because it was relatively quiet. Needless to say, she experienced loads of excitement the night that I had you. She was telling all of her visitors that the lady in Room 311 had her baby in the elevator! I felt like a freak and was so relieved when I could finally come home."

By this point, we were laughing so hard and so loud that we were in tears. Jim felt that his birth preordained him in the role of being the clown, and the rest of us ribbed him as families tend to do. The laughter was a much needed relief to a difficult situation.

Believe it or not, I still have the hat that I was wearing when Jim was born. It is the centerpiece of my collection.

C.R.

Typo-Laughical Errors

The statue showed that David was a worrier.

Pulitz Surprise.

Homer will be in rear form today.

She walked on pre-Madonna legs.

From papers presented to tutors in the CAI Lab

26

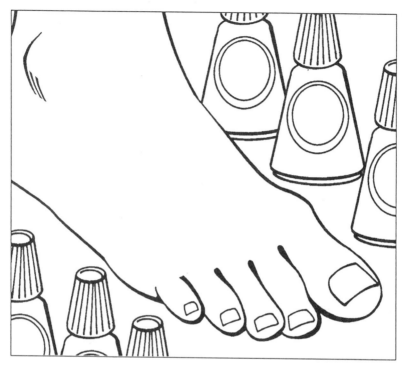

Grandma's Toenails

If we can't maintain our perspective about the minor problems in our life, we'll never be able to handle the disasters. This was brought home to me last December.

Every once in a while I indulge myself by getting a pedicure. I go to a little shop where all the employees are Vietnamese and they only do manicures and pedicures.

The pedicure itself isn't all that great, because the manicurist is very often merciless. I sometimes feel the tools of her trade are rose pruners and a trowel, but it's hard to complain to a person who smiles so sweetly. When I think about what she must have gone through to get to

27

this country, I hate to be a whiner. Mainly, I go because I love the feeling of being pampered and the foot and ankle massage that goes with the pedicure is wonderful.

On this particular occasion, I took my seven-year-old grandson, Joey, with me. When it came time to choose the polish for my toes, Joey begged to pick out the color. I am basically a clear polish person, but I said, "Sure."

Joey's first choice was midnight blue, then purple, then black. I was appalled. I couldn't wear those colors on my toes! Joey was noticeably disappointed at my rejections, but finally settled on a light pink that I found acceptable.

Later, I thought, 'Anita, what is the matter with you? What difference could it possibly make what color he picked? No one even has to see your toenails. Your shoes will hide them, and if you really hate the color, there's always polish remover.'

The big problem would have been if he wanted to wear the polish on his own toenails.

So, the next time I went for my pedicure, I made it a point to take Joey along and let him choose the color. He was thrilled. Since then, I have had midnight blue toenails, purple toenails, and black toenails. In fact, as I write this, I have lime green toenails.

You know what? Those toenails don't hurt a bit. And I am one of the most fortunate grandmothers. I have a grandson who thinks I have the most beautiful feet in the world.

A.C.M.

The Garbage Day

The garbage truck! I hear it coming in the distance and my mind goes wild. Do the boys have the garbage out? I didn't hear the can lids rattle last night. I don't hear any shuffling of cans in the garage now! As the intermittent screech of the truck breaks gets closer, my heart races! Why do I get so charged when I hear that grinding noise of garbage being mashed? Will all my garbage be in that truck soon or will it continue to pile up in the basement and kitchen, smelling until the next pick-up day?

Oh, I can't wait any longer. I must get up now and see

what decision must be made! First, I must see whose day it is to take the garbage out. The list is always posted with each of the five boy's names. Next, I must see if I can rally "the son of the day" to beat the garbage truck to our stop. If he misses, will he have to store the garbage in his room? If he's left for work or school will I have to put the bags in his bed? How surprised he'll be when he gets home to find garbage in his bed!

Maybe I'll be surprised and find out the garbage has already been taken out! Yes! What a thrill it is to hear the big truck grind to a screeching halt at our stop and know that our garbage is being mashed next to our neighbor's trash.

T.W.

Typo-Laughical Errors

"The Nutcracker" is a very pieceful piece of music.

I received a music lesion as a child.

I was furious when I got a run in my panty hoes.

Children use adults as their road models.

Her personal qualities were the crowing achievement of nature.

We sat around a bomb fire.

From papers presented to tutors in the CAI Lab

Dining Room Wallpaper

It's been so many years ago, but it's still fresh in my mind. I was the prototype of the harried house wife and then some.

When this story occurred our family consisted of four boys. The oldest, Hayes, was nine; the second, Andy, was eight; Jim was six and Sam was two years old.

One day I was running errands with Sam. The other three were at home with the housekeeper.

Upon my return home I noticed someone had taken a knife and made terrible gauges in the gorgeous silk dining room wallpaper. I, of course, became very upset and began questioning the boys about who was responsible. After a

31

week it became obvious there were no confessions forth-
coming although one son had inquired about the
punishment.

We had dinner in the dining room the night before I was
going to the hospital the next day for surgery. I wanted to
leave things on an up note. We proposed forgetting all
about this unfortunate event on the condition that on the
day each son turned 21 he was to call home and admit or
deny responsibility. We never really thought such a thing
would ever happen...

When Hayes turned 21, he was a student at Vanderbilt.
We called to wish him a happy birthday and he informed us
he hadn't done it.

Andy called practically at dawn the day of his 21st
birthday. He was grateful that he didn't have to call from
Vietnam and he confessed that he hadn't done it either. The
odds had now changed.

Eighteen months after Andy turned 21, it was Jim's
birthday. That day was so hot and humid. I was tired and
I told Emma, our housekeeper, that I had promised Jim I
would come and see him play a tennis match. I didn't want
to go, but I had promised. Jim was one of the better
players in town, but this day he was trounced. As he
walked off the court I was thinking, "Good, I can go home
now."

I said. "Hi Jim"

He replied, "O.K. I did it."

It was the furthest thing from my mind. We laughed
and laughed. We still laugh today. Our family joke has
continued to be remembered for 15 years.

{By the way, it was Jim who asked about the
punishment! I knew he was the culprit from the beginning.}

L.M.

100 Uses for a Younger Brother

Have you ever wondered what you could do with your younger brother? Well, I just happen to have two younger brothers myself, so I'm an expert on the topic. I know a hundred uses for a younger brother!

Almost everybody has to run errands every now and then. I bet a lot of people don't like to run errands. Well, here's a use for a younger brother. You can make him run all of your errands!

That would probably be very nice. Say you had to go to the grocery store and get some bread for your Mom. You didn't want to go because you wanted to go to your friend's house. So you called your brother and said, "Do you want to go to the grocery store and get some bread for Mom? If you do, Mom will be really proud of you!

"Well, ... Okay. I'll go," your brother says! Now you can go to your friend's house!

Here is a second use for a younger brother. You could make your younger brother dance or do something else entertaining for you when you're bored. If your favorite show on T.V. is over and you don't want to play a game, it's time for some entertainment! Call your brother into the room, turn on some music, and ask your brother to dance. What he'll probably do is start moving to the beat of music and maybe even try to sing along with it. When he gets tired of dancing, maybe he'll do something else entertaining. Maybe he will tell jokes or something! That would be neat!

Now here's an unusual use for a younger brother ... you could use him for a table! If you picked a nice bouquet of flowers and didn't have any place to put it, you could say to your brother, "Bend over for a minute and get on your hands and knees." He would get on his hands and knees and you would put the flowers on his back.

"Get them off me!", he would yell.

"No, I think I'll leave them on for a little while," I would reply.

So, of course he would have to stay on his hands and knees until I took the flowers off because if he stood up he would break the vase that the flowers were in and he would get in big trouble.

The next use is he would keep secrets. If you did something you weren't supposed to do and your brother saw you, you could say, "Hey, listen. I know I'm doing something wrong here. Don't tell Mom or else I'll get in trouble for doing it and you'll get in trouble for being a tattletale."

Then your brother will say, "Okay, I won't tell because I don't want to get in trouble."

I don't think he would add, "I don't want you to get in trouble either," but if he is in a good, good mood he might!

Another use is your younger brother could carry all of your stuff. Here is a good example. You and your brother go to the same school. You're in 4th grade and he is in 1st grade. All he has to carry is a very small backpack. You have to carry a bigger backpack and some thick, fat books. "Hey, can you help me carry my stuff?" you ask your brother.

"Sure," he answers. "I'll take your stuff and you take my stuff." You tell him.

"All right," he says as he hands you his little backpack.

You give him your stuff and he says, "Boy this sure is heavy," and he carries your stuff all the way to school!

You could also persuade your younger brother to buy something you want with his money. Pretend that you are at a bookstore and you see this really neat book. Unfortunately, you have already spent your money. You call your brother and show him the book. You tell him that it is a really cool book. He looks at it and says, "Well ... I'll get it." Now you've gotten both the books that you wanted.

Well, it's time for me to go and I don't think I've quite covered 100 uses for a younger brother, but if I could stay and tell them to you all day I could probably cover 100 uses. I know all of my suggestions are funny, but I wouldn't trade my two younger brothers for a million, billion dollars!

M.K., Age 10
Winner of Jassmine County, KY's Speech Contest for Fourth Graders

Just Charge It!

After losing my mother, I now know that one of the most stressful events in life is the death of a parent. Although I tried to tell myself that I was prepared for it, I was devastated at not only losing a parent, but also my best friend. Still, a person tries to find many ways to cope with this situation and humor can be one of them.

When we went to the funeral home to make the arrangements, we discussed having two viewings - one in the city where my parents live, and the other one in her hometown, which was out of state. What became funny to us was that the funeral home was going to fly the body from one state to another, and my mother was afraid of flying. We all decided that she would come back to haunt us because we were letting her be flown.

My mother was an avid shopper and bargain hunter. Some of my fondest memories of her are of the two of us out shopping together. While going through her things I found an old credit card that she had used many times. I decided to put it in her hand at the funeral home viewings. This gave us something cheerful to talk about after people had offered their condolences. I also put a head scarf underneath the coverlet in the casket because she had always wore one when she went out of the house; she had often told me that I would be healthier if I wore scarves (which I never do).

Throughout the whole funeral process, I tried to focus on the happy times Mother had with her family and friends. This helped me get though a very difficult time.

J.P.

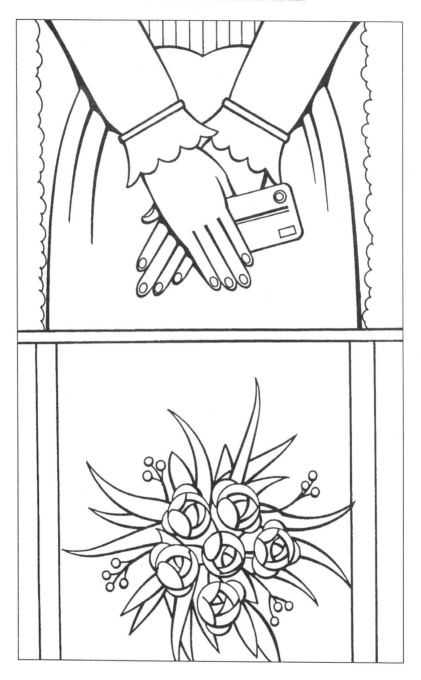

I Didn't Catch the Bridal Bouquet Either!

In the past, I have had the good fortune of having my life lessons show up in the form of men. One particular man decided that the only way to end our relationship, and my amazing ability to attach myself to him like a glue stick, was to be direct. He quite pointedly informed me that "I was not good enough for him!"

There were images of devastation...bleak existence... food deprivation...(not for long, thank goodness), and just your basic battle with low self-esteem and self-worth. What was I to do?

I could try the old standby...total withdrawal to a reclusive sanctuary of self-loathing, sleepless nights, and pitiful self-talk. I even tried to be creative. I attempted to tearfully mold myself into the shape of my well-worn corduroy couch. That weft can be monstrous on your face.

Well, time passed and I came to my senses. Not only was I good enough for me..I was spectacular!

Happy ending time! Said man married someone else — whew! On that wonderful day, I had the pleasure of doing my stand-up comedy routine at their wedding reception!

I was able to laugh in the face of adversity, literally and figuratively. In front of everybody (and me), I was able to stand up inside of myself. Not good enough? Wrong! I am spectacular!

D.W.

A Tisket, A Tasket, A Humor Basket

"Hello, Mr. Jones. My name is Cathy and I am your evening nurse," I said with a smile.

After I did my vital signs and assessments, I giggled as I realized I must look like a Christmas tree to him. Around my neck dangled my stethoscope, a roll of silk tape, and a glow-in-the-dark green coil with the narcotic keys. Bulging out of my hip pockets were sterile needles, alcohol wipes, scissors, kelly clamp, and pieces of paper. I assured Mr. Jones that if he needed anything I was probably wearing it; but if I wasn't I could get it! I also had all kinds of goodies in my basket for him.

About three years ago, I became aware of how many patients (and sometimes visitors) had nothing to do to help pass the time. That prompted me to assemble my first humor basket. After a colleague wove a basket, I filled it with items appropriate to my patients. It contained stamped note cards, windup toys, Pokey and Gumby dolls, a deck of cards, a small photo album with seasonal photographs, some joke books, huge bright yellow sunglasses and a terrific rubber chicken.

Patients enjoy this extra personal touch. I believe it provides them with a brief respite from their struggle with illness.

A patient in traction enjoyed the basket, especially the red rubber lobster that crawled when squeezed. She would hide it under the covers by her leg. When the doctors made rounds in the morning, (scores of them!), she

would say something is gnawing at my leg, pull up the covers, and everyone would have a wonderful laugh!!

Another patient who worked in a quarry loved the fake granite rock. He would throw it at friends when they came to visit!

One patient commented, "Thanks for the laughs; my staples needed those!"

C. J.

You Can't Get There From Here

Immediately prior to making an out of state presentation, I had spent ten days in meditation and reflection in a retreat. I was feeling disconnected a bit which became more evident as I traveled to St. Louis.

When I arrived in the St. Louis airport, I found that no one was there to meet me. I travel a lot giving talks so I have a basic rule I operate from...if there's no one to meet me, the place must be close enough to reach by cab. So I went out and told the cab driver I wanted to go to the Holiday Inn in Cape Girardeau, MO. He said, "Lady, that is over two hours from here. It's at the other end of the state!"

I was feeling a little irritated and certainly abandoned. I was going to have to rent a car and drive those two plus hours.

Coming back into the terminal, I spotted a limousine driver. I asked him who he was waiting for. He responded with, "Who are you?" I'm from New York and who was he to ask me that? I responded with, "Who are you waiting for!?!" He said a name and of course, it wasn't me. He softened a bit and said, "Where are you trying to go?"

I told him and he said there's a lady over there waiting for a limousine to Cape Girardeau. I went over and introduced myself and suggested we share the limo. She said, "Fine. But I've been waiting an hour and it still hasn't come." I said, "I'll call because I need to add my name."

When I called I found out that they didn't have her on

any reservation list. I made reservations for both of us and we began to wait. We waited over an hour before the limousine arrived and then came the two hour drive to Cape Girardeau.

I finally arrived at the hotel at midnight, I was tired, irritated about the lack of communication. I was also worried about the return trip. I decided to check my return flight time to see if I had enough time for the trip back. In my packet of airline tickets I found a ticket for a connecting flight from St. Louis to Cape Girardeau. I was supposed to have caught another plane!

They hadn't forgotten me. I laughed and the next morning told the story to my audience. They laughed and the more we laughed the better it felt.

J.Q.

Let there Be Light

I am a professional nurse who works with staff and patients every day. I enjoy my career and feel competent. I'm always trying to learn more and broaden my knowledge of nursing.

I was flattered and excited when I was asked to be one of the moderators of a major nursing research conference. My duties included meeting the speakers and assisting them with any particular needs they had for their presentations.

When I welcomed my first speaker and eagerly inquired if there was anything she needed for her talk the next day, she said,

"Yes, there is. I need a pointer, you know, a flashlight."

I replied that I'd get right on it. I asked some of the other staff but no one had a flashlight.

Two things that nurses do very well are meet others needs and problem solve in creative ways. When I arrived at home that evening I was still worried about getting my speaker a flashlight to point with. Then I remembered we had a small, compact flashlight. I found it, went out and got new batteries. I went to bed a happy person.

The next day just as I was about to produce my clever solution, one of my colleagues commented that it was a shame we didn't have one of those pointers that produced a light beam! Within the next ten seconds my emotions ranged from acute embarrassment at my naivete, to frustration that I'd spent all that time on problem solving to immense relief that I hadn't produced the flashlight (with extra batteries)!

Then I found myself laughing. My "solution" became the hit of the conference. We all had mental pictures of the speaker pointing a flashlight on her slides.

B. W.

A Real Fish Story

Since the crisis of Barry's suicide in 1987, humor seems to come more easily.

I recall dreading the finality of the funeral service and found myself edging toward the exit to escape. The sight of the pallbearers, all dear friends, rescued me. Seeing them dressed so somberly struck me funny and I told them that I should have gotten fish ties for them to wear. Barry would have had a hoot over that.

We laughed hysterically while those around us stared in disapproval, thinking it quite inappropriate for the widow

to be laughing just seconds prior to the eulogy.

My children displayed collages of photos around the closed casket which depicted Barry in amusing situations. This brought back many loving memories of the warm, funny man we loved.

Visitors, many of whom I did not know, each had a humorous story to relate about Barry, a man who loved to entertain people. It was extremely cathartic to laugh and cry with so many who loved him.

My friends, children and I still love to recall his funny antics.

B.C.

Help Me, I'm Depressed and I Can't Get Up

For seventeen years, my mother took care of my invalid father at home. For twelve of those years, he was totally bedridden.

Mom bathed Dad, shaved him, fed him, dressed him, changed his diapers, did everything for him. Only during the last two years did she have live-in help after she had

destroyed her knees by lifting Dad into and out of bed. But in those seventeen years Dad spent no time in a convalescent hospital, nor did he ever get a bed sore!

It's not hard to imagine how depressing this situation would be. It was especially hard to see my dear mother deteriorating in physical health as well as spirit as she cared for this man she had loved with all her heart for so many years.

But even in the midst of all this, Mom still showed flashes of humor for which she was known in our family. It may have been gallows humor, but humor it was.

One day I was talking to Mom on the phone.

She related, "You know, I was so depressed yesterday. I almost called that Suicide Hot Line. But I didn't know if they would help me on the phone, or come out to the house and show me how to do it!"

A.C.M.

My, He Looks Good!

Grandpa had been a farmer all his life. He had never worn a suit of clothes. All of his life he had worn overalls. He wore them to work in the fields, to go to town on market day and to visit neighbors. On Sundays he wore clean, pressed overalls and a clean shirt to church services.

When Grandpa died the family decided to lay him out in a store bought, brand new suit of clothes. He wasn't going to his reward in overalls.

As the visitors and family began to arrive for visitation, they were all impressed with how good Grandpa looked in his suit of clothes.

"My, don't he look wonderful. That suit sure is special"

"I can't believe the difference that suit makes."

As the evening wore on someone suggested that they take a picture of Grandpa because he looked so good. Uncle Ed went home and got his camera with a wide angle lens.

The family all began discussing what kind of picture they wanted. It was finally decided it should be a family portrait!!

They took Grandpa out of the coffin, leaned him in a corner with all the family on either side grinning. One of the little granddaughters who was wearing a frilly dress was seated at Grandpa's feet to disguise the fact that he didn't have any shoes on.

This picture is a family treasure.

A.

49

Also by Ann Weeks:

- ...And Then There Were Nine
- Nothing Serious...Just a little chat with the boss
- All I Needed To Know About The Holidays I Learned From Santa Claus
- More Than Music
- Creativity and Leadership (video)
- Humor and Healing (audiocassette)